For

THE SPORTS PAGE

QUOTATIONS ON BASEBALL, FOOTBALL, GOLF & OTHER SPORTS

COMPILED BY
PETER BEILENSON

DESIGN BY
MULLEN & KATZ

PETER PAUPER PRESS, INC.
WHITE PLAINS · NEW YORK

For Valerie, Alex, and Jane,
good sports, with love

Peter Pauper Press, Inc.
202 Mamaroneck Avenue
White Plains, NY 10601

ISBN 0-88088-256-5
Library of Congress No. 89-60649
Printed in China
13 12 11 10 9 8 7

Persons in this book are identified in most cases by their positions at the time the statements were made.

CONTENTS

GOLF

If a lot of people gripped a knife and fork like they do a golf club, they'd starve to death.

SAM SNEAD

Thinking must be the hardest thing we do in golf, because we do so little of it.

HARVEY PENICK

Playing golf is not hot work.
Cutting sugar cane for a dollar a day
is hot work.

CHI CHI RODRIGUEZ

The income tax has made liars out of more Americans than golf.

WILL ROGERS

When I am asked what is the biggest break I ever had in golf, I say it is when the IRS transferred my dad from the Dallas office to Austin. Because I arrived in Austin at age 13 to encounter Mr. [Harvey] Penick and Ben Crenshaw. In my wildest dreams I couldn't have hoped for a finer teacher or stronger competition.

TOM KITE

To me, the basics mean making a smooth swing, hitting the fairway, hitting the green, making a smooth stroke, and sinking the birdie putt.

ERNIE ELS

We all choke. You're not human if you haven't. We get just as nervous as the average guy playing for the club championship.

CURTIS STRANGE

Ben {Hogan} was tough. But I enjoyed playing with him. He never said anything and let me concentrate on my game.

SAM SNEAD

There's no such thing as natural touch. Touch is something you create by hitting millions of golf balls.

LEE TREVINO

When I look back on my career, I was really lucky. I learned to play from Nelson and Hogan, which is like learning to paint from Michelangelo and Leonardo. How's it get better than that?

KEN VENTURI

Money was never a goal for me because of my amateur training. I was taught to win, and that was it.

JOANNE CARNER

I have been trying to figure out what the little thing is that makes one person better [as a golfer] than another. The only thing I can think of is that I'm not afraid to lose and I'm not afraid to win.

PATTY SHEEHAN

She [Judy Rankin] is so small, she might get lost in an unreplaced divot.

BOB TOSKI

I like the competition, but those [major] tournaments are tough. The crowds are so huge and the people line up so close on either side, it really puts pressure on a high handicapper. You're scared to death you're going to kill somebody.

GEORGE BUSH

You all know Jerry Ford—the most dangerous driver since Ben Hur.

BOB HOPE

A lot more people beat me now.

DWIGHT D. EISENHOWER,

explaining what happened to his golf game after leaving the White House

A decision of the courts decided that the game of golf may be played on Sunday, not being a game within the view of the law, but being a form of moral effort.

STEPHEN LEACOCK

They say golf builds character. You could do better by going to church and save money in the bargain. Tithing is chump change compared with what we blow on golf.

PETER ANDREWS

I'm the best. I just haven't played yet.

MUHAMMAD ALI,

when asked about his golf game

Golf and sex are about the only things you can enjoy without being good at.

JIMMY DEMARET

Sam {Snead} doesn't know a dam' thing about the golf swing.
But he does it better than anyone else.

BEN HOGAN

Golf: a game in which you claim the privileges of age, and retain the playthings of childhood.

SAMUEL JOHNSON

I regard golf as an expensive way of playing marbles.

G. K. CHESTERTON

It is impossible to imagine Goethe or Beethoven being good at billiards or golf.

H. L. MENCKEN

I don't say my golf game is bad, but if I grew tomatoes, they'd come up sliced.

MILLER BARBER

Playing in the U.S. Open is like tippy-toeing through hell.

JERRY MCGEE

I hate drawing attention to myself. I'm terribly uncomfortable being on display. My ideal tournament would be to ambush the field on the last day, even the last hole, and win when nobody knew I'd even been there all week.

BRUCE LIETZKE

I do much of my creative thinking while golfing, If people know you are working at home they think nothing of walking in for a cup of coffee. But they wouldn't dream of interrupting you on the golf course.

HARPER LEE,

writer

A sick appendix
is not as difficult to deal with
as a five-foot putt.

GENE SARAZEN

Golf is a good walk spoiled.

MARK TWAIN

[I consider myself an athlete] because
I play a game with a ball and a stick
and get paid handsomely to do it.
The only thing I don't do is go out on strike.

MARK McCUMBER

One of the advantages bowling has over golf is
that you seldom lose a bowling ball.

DON CARTER,

bowling great

Golf seems to me an arduous way
to go for a walk.
I prefer to take the dogs out.

PRINCESS ANNE

Golf is not a sport.
Golf is men in ugly pants, walking.
ROSIE O'DONNELL

If you watch a game, it's fun.
If you play it, it's recreation.
If you work at it, it's golf.
BOB HOPE

If you can't enjoy the times
in between the golf shots, then you're
going to have a pretty difficult life,
because most of your life is the time
spent in between.
PETER JACOBSEN

May I live long enough to shoot my age.
GOLFER'S PRAYER

Years ago we discovered the exact point,
the dead center of middle age.
It occurs when you are too young
to take up golf and too old
to rush up to the net.

FRANKLIN P. ADAMS

Do you want to know the difference
between golf and tennis?
Tennis is murderous.
You want to kill your opponent.
But golf is suicide.
You want to kill yourself.

BRENDAN GILL

TENNIS

I strongly believe that
any sport thrives on rivalries.
Rivalry is what creates interest.
It creates a passion for the sport.

ANDRE AGASSI

I am looking forward to
beating his brains
the next time I play him.

PETE SAMPRAS,
on archrival Andre Agassi

I'll kick Pete's a… .

ANDRE AGASSI

It's unbelievable;
for a long time everything was dark,
and now I see the sun.
It's great to be playing tennis again.

MONICA SELES,
after her physical and emotional receovery from a knife wound

He is not as fast at the net as he used to be.
It was a little sad.
He's older than he was five years ago,
that's for sure.

MICHAEL STICH,
German star, on Stefan Edberg

To play against him,
you feel like a small moth
against a big elephant.

YEVGENY KAFELNIKOV,
on clay court master Thomas Muster

Tennis is a thinking man's game,
and the Chinese, who value cleverness,
respond to that. In that sense,
maybe my background helps my tennis.
Overall, my best asset is the ability to
move quickly and to think clearly,
often at the same time.

MICHAEL CHANG,

Chinese-American tennis star

I've been in the twilight of my career longer
than most people have had careers.

MARTINA NAVRATILOVA

I think in France we live too well,
and sometimes that shows on the court.
Our players don't have enough aggressiveness.
Sometimes we French lack guts.

FRANCOISE DURR

[My teachers] know I'm not ditching.

LINDSAY DAVENPORT,

on missing high school classes

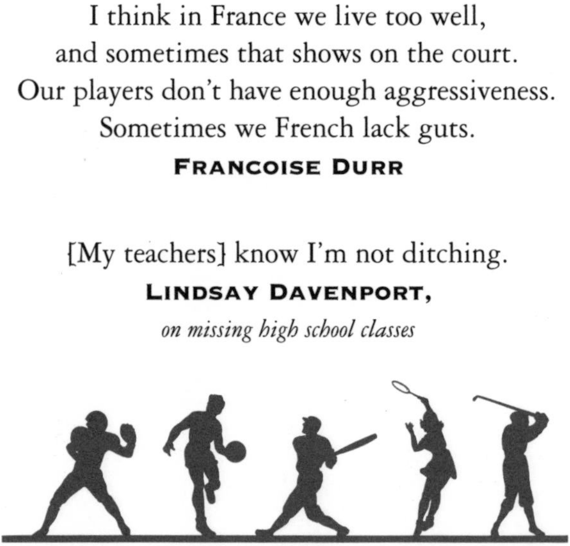

Chris Evert never threw a tantrum,
groused at opponents or blamed officials.
A bad call produced a steely stare at most.
Chris behaved like an adult, taking
full responsibility for her
performance and deportment.

CAMILLE PAGLIA,

writer

The speed is a lot more impressive live.

MARTINA HINGIS,

on the difference between playing Steffi Graf and watching her on television

It is sickening that someone who is
down-to-earth, polite, behaves well, is
reasonably clever and wears nice clothes almost
has to apologize for being the way he is.

IVAN LENDL,

on his colleague, Pete Sampras

The older I get, the better I used to be.

BRAD GILBERT

For years I felt underappreciated, and now I feel overappreciated. I hit an average shot and get a standing ovation. I think they go a little overboard, but I can take it.

MARTINA NAVRATILOVA,

on reaction from fans during her last year on the women's singles tour

Ideal tennis is a match that I don't regret.

KIMIKO DATE,

Japanese star

I think I'm really taking a good look at the big picture. That's the difference between being around for the final or watching the final from my sofa at home.

ANDRE AGASSI

I just like needed something like to yell out or something. I didn't want to start spazzing out so I yelled at the crow.

JENNIFER CAPRIATI,

explaining why she yelled "shut up" at a bird during a match

Tennis adds years to your life
and life to your years.

ROY WILDER

Being champion is all well and good,
but you can't eat a crown.

ALTHEA GIBSON DARBON,
on her retirement from tennis

Tennis is a perfect combination of
violent action taking place in an
atmosphere of total tranquillity.

BILLIE JEAN KING

I think self-awareness is probably
the most important thing towards
being a champion.

BILLIE JEAN KING

The problem is that when you get [experience],
you're too damned old to do anything about it.

JIMMY CONNORS

I hate to lose more than I like to win.
I hate to see the happiness on their faces
when they beat me.

JIMMY CONNORS

Everybody loves success,
but they hate successful people.

JOHN MCENROE

It is vital, in my opinion,
that tennis maintains a
strong and watchful stand
against swearing.

JOHN MCENROE,
infamous for his court demeanor

Winners aren't popular.
Losers often are.

VIRGINIA WADE,
English tennis star

THE OLYMPICS

The important thing in the Olympic Games
is not to win, but to take part;
the important thing in life is not the triumph
but the struggle; the essential thing is
not to have conquered but to have fought well.

BARON DE COUBERTIN,

founder of the modern Olympics

Sir, you are the greatest athlete in the world.

KING GUSTAV V OF SWEDEN,

to Jim Thorpe at the 1912 Olympics in Stockholm

Thanks, King.

JIM THORPE

You should be able to do your entire routine sound asleep in your pajamas without one mistake.

MARY LOU RETTON,

first American woman to win an individual gold medal in gymnastics

When I came into the stadium and saw all the colors and everything, I told myself, "Listen, just look straight ahead, because if you don't you're probably going to faint."

JOAN BENOIT,

American marathoner, on her gold medal-winning performance in the 1984 Los Angeles Summer Olympics

I ski to win. When the day comes that I can't get myself into a fighting mood anymore, I won't be able to win and I'll stop racing.

INGEMAR STENMARK

To win you have to risk loss.

JEAN-CLAUDE KILLY,

French skier

I always have good finishes.
You go as hard as you can until the end.
You can always rest when it's over.

JANET EVANS,

American swimmer

I very often have the following urge:
I suddenly feel on the street that I have to run.
I absolutely have to run, dressed in a suit,
wearing my hat and tie, not paying attention
to the passers-by. . . . Then convention gets
the upper hand and I restrain myself.

VALERY BORZOV,

Ukrainian sprinter

They [emotions] should be bottled up inside.
You want it to come out on the track.

EVELYN ASHFORD

There is no greater glory for a man
as long as he lives than that which he wins
by his own hands and feet.

HOMER,

The Odyssey

I wanted no part of politics, and I wasn't in Berlin to compete against any one athlete. The purpose of the Olympics, anyway, was to do your best. As I'd learned long ago . . . the only victory that counts is the one over yourself.

JESSE OWENS,

on the 1936 Olympics in Hitler's Germany

It was the best managed and attended big affair you ever saw. Seeing or reading about the exploits of the youth of the whole world for the last few weeks has been a good thing for everybody.

WILL ROGERS,

on the beneficial effects of the 1932 Olympics in Los Angeles, during a worldwide depression

The key is knowing how to peak.

LASSE VIREN,

Finnish long distance runner

Compete against yourself, not others.

PEGGY FLEMING,

American figure skater

My attitude is never to be satisfied, never enough, never. The girls, they must be little tigers, clawing, kicking, biting, roaring to the top. They stop for one minute—poof!—they are finished.

BELA KAROLYI,

gymnastics coach

Don't be frightened if things seem difficult in the beginning . . . The important thing is not to retreat; you have to master yourself. This ability to conquer oneself is no doubt the most precious of all the things sports bestows upon us.

OLGA KORBUT,

Russian gymnast

I felt like angels were lifting and spinning me.

BRIAN BOITANO,

winner of the gold medal in the 1988 Calgary Winter Olympics

I finally put it together. You want your best performance to be at the Olympic Games.

GREG LOUGANIS,

on his winning performance in platform diving at the 1984 Olympics

Achievement is difficult.
It requires enormous effort.
Those who can work through the struggle are the ones who are going to be successful.

JACKIE JOYNER-KERSEE,

American track star

The victor all his remaining days breathes a delicious and serene air when he remembers the Games.

PINDAR,

commenting on the ancient Games in 476 B.C.

I want only to perform honorably.

EMIL ZATOPEK,

Czech runner, prior to running and winning his first-ever marathon, at the 1952 Olympics in Helsinki

Rejoice, we conquer.

PHEIDIPPIDES,

Greek runner who, legend has it, ran across the plains of Marathon, to carry news of a military victory to the people of Athens, before dying

Only think of two things—the report of the pistol and the tape. When you hear the one, just run like hell till you break the other.

SAM MUSSABINI,

coaching Harold Abrahams (portrayed in the film **Chariots of Fire***) prior to his winning the 100 meters in the 1924 Olympics*

Looking back, I should have pushed her, but the headlines tomorrow would have read "Decker pushes Zola."

MARY DECKER,

after a controversial collision with Zola Budd during the 3,000 meters in the Los Angeles Olympics which resulted in an injury to Decker and a poor finish for Budd

I do not like to be beaten.

ERIC LIDDELL,

*Scotsman, running colleague of Harold Abrahams (also portrayed in **Chariots of Fire**)*

When I looked from the top of the jump,
I was so frightened that my bum
shriveled up like a prune.

MICHAEL "EDDIE THE EAGLE" EDWARDS,

English ski jumper who placed last in the 1988 competition in Calgary

If I work on a certain move constantly, then, finally, it doesn't seem so risky to me. The move stays dangerous and looks dangerous to my foes, but not to me. Hard work has made it easy. That is my secret. That is why I win.

NADIA COMANECI,

Romanian gymnast

Citius, altius, fortius [faster, higher, stronger].

OLYMPIC MOTTO,

coined for the 1924 summer games in Paris by French schoolmaster R. P. Didon

BASEBALL

You can take a nap in between
{Dodgers pitcher Hideo Nomo's} pitches.

GARY SHEFFIELD,

Marlins outfielder

I'd go through hell in a gasoline suit
to play baseball.

PETE ROSE

Us ball players do things backward.
First we play, then we retire and go to work.

CHARLIE GEHRINGER,

Hall of Fame second baseman

The good Lord was good to me. He gave me a strong body, a good right arm, and a weak mind.

DIZZY DEAN

Don't look back.
Someone might be gaining on you.

LEROY (SATCHEL) PAIGE

Baseball is too much of a sport to be called a business, and too much of a business to be called a sport.

PHILIP K. WRIGLEY,
Chicago Cubs owner

Your body is just like a bar of soap.
It gradually wears down from repeated use.

DICK ALLEN

When you're hitting the ball, it comes at you looking like a grapefruit. When you're not, it looks like a black-eyed pea.

GEORGE SCOTT,
Boston Red Sox

Why pitch nine innings when you can get
just as famous pitching two?

SPARKY LYLE,

N.Y. Yankees relief pitcher

My favorite play is the hit-and-run.
See who's covering [second]
and hit a ground ball where he was.

TONY GWYNN,

San Diego Padres

There's nothing mysterious about winning.
It's a matter of executing the fundamentals.

CAL RIPKEN,

Baltimore Orioles "iron man" shortstop

The Giants win the pennant!
The Giants win the pennant! I don't believe it—
the Giants win the pennant!

RUSS HODGES,

radio broadcaster, after the Giants' Bobby Thompson hit the "Shot Heard Round the World" to win the 1951 NL Playoff with the Brooklyn Dodgers

If somebody came up and hit .450, stole 100 bases and performed a miracle in the field every day I'd still look you in the eye and say Willie {Mays} was better. He could do the five things you have to do to be a superstar: hit, hit with power, run, throw and field. And he had that other magic ingredient that turns a superstar into a super superstar. He lit up the room when he came in. He was a joy to be around.

LEO DUROCHER,

N.Y. Giants manager

I'm no different from anyone else with two arms, two legs, and forty-two-hundred hits.

PETE ROSE

A homer a day will boost my pay.

JOSH GIBSON,

Negro Leagues great

How can I hit and think at the same time?

YOGI BERRA

I believe that racial extractions and color hues and forms of worship become secondary to what men can do. The American public is not as concerned with a first baseman's pigmentation as it is with the power of his swing, the dexterity of his slide, and the gracefulness of his fielding or the speed of his legs.

BRANCH RICKEY,

who broke baseball's color barrier by bringing Jackie Robinson to the Dodgers

I'm not concerned with your liking or disliking me. . . . All I ask is that you respect me as a human being.

JACKIE ROBINSON

The most important things are location and knowing how to pitch. If you can't do those things up here, you can't win. It's as simple as that. You can forget about good stuff and you can forget about radar guns. If you can't locate your pitches, you can't win. Period.

LOU PINIELLA,

Mariners manager

All I can tell 'em is pick a good one and sock it. I get back to the dugout and they ask me what it was I hit and I tell 'em I don't know except it looked good.

BABE RUTH

[The secret of my success is] clean living and a fast outfield.

LEFTY GOMEZ

I always eat frog legs before I pitch. It makes my fastball jump.

RICK RICE,

Baltimore Orioles pitcher

It wasn't just that he hit more home runs than anybody else, he hit them better, higher, farther, with more theatrical timing and a more flamboyant flourish. Nobody could strike out like Babe Ruth. Nobody circled the bases with the same pigeon-toed, mincing majesty.

RED SMITH

I hit 'em where they ain't.

WEE WILLIE KEELER

I never blame myself when I'm not hitting. I just blame the bat, and if it keeps up I change bats. After all, if I know it isn't my fault that I'm not hitting, how can I get mad at myself?

YOGI BERRA

When you see the ball,
you have a better idea where it is.

JEFF TORBORG,

White Sox manager

When I started, it [baseball] was played by nine tough competitors on grass in graceful ball parks. By the time I was finished, there were 10 men on each side, the game was played indoors, on plastic, and I had to spend half of my time watching out for a man dressed in a chicken suit who kept trying to kiss me.

RON LUCIANO,

American League umpire

Cubs fans are 90 percent scar tissue.

GEORGE WILL

I became a good pitcher when I stopped trying to make them miss the ball and started trying to make them hit it.

SANDY KOUFAX

[Greg Maddux's] kind of talent usually comes with an ego sidecar. He doesn't have it. He's as easygoing as the guy next door.

JOHN SCHUERHOLZ,

Atlanta Braves general manager

Sure, I have muffed a few in my time. But I never called one wrong in my heart.

BILL KLEM,

umpire

It took 15 years to get you out of a game.
Sometimes I'm out in 15 minutes.

LEFTY GOMEZ,

to Lou Gehrig after illness forced Gehrig out of the line-up

Fans, for the past two weeks you have been reading about what a bad break I got. Yet today I consider myself the luckiest man on the face of the earth.

LOU GEHRIG,

on his "day" at Yankee Stadium, two years before his death

A good professional athlete must have the love of a little boy. And the good players feel the kind of love for the game that they did when they were Little Leaguers.

TOM SEAVER

FOOTBALL

In life as in a football game,
the principle to follow is: Hit the line hard.

THEODORE ROOSEVELT

I love football. I really love football.
As far as I'm concerned, it's the second best
thing in the world.

JOE NAMATH

Coach, some day when the going gets rough, tell
the boys to win one for the Gipper.

GEORGE GIPP,
on his deathbed, to Knute Rockne

MERIAL PREMIER[SM]

I can say with a clear conscience that I have never knowingly bit another football player. For one thing, I believe in good hygiene.

CONRAD DOBLER,

in response to charges that he had bitten a rival player

I had pro offers from the Detroit Lions and Green Bay Packers, who were pretty hard up for linemen in those days. If I had gone into professional football the name Jerry Ford might have been a household word today.

GERALD FORD,

when serving as Vice-President

We're basically a save-the-whales team; we can't turn down big people who can play.

GEORGE YOUNG,

N.Y. Giants general manager

Is it normal to wake up in the morning in a sweat because you can't wait to beat another human's guts out?

JOE KAPP,

Minnesota Vikings quarterback

Pro football is like nuclear warfare.
There are no winners, only survivors.

FRANK GIFFORD

You have to decide if the experience you will
have is worth the pain you will feel.

JACK YOUNGBLOOD,

L.A. Rams defensive end

If you can't explain it,
how can you take credit for it?

HAROLD "RED" GRANGE,

Chicago Bears halfback, on his talent for eluding tacklers

Rugby is a beastly game played by gentlemen;
soccer is a gentleman's game played by beasts;
football is a beastly game played by beasts.

HENRY BLAHA

There is no such animal
as a cornerback who hasn't gotten burned.

DEION SANDERS,

cornerback for the Atlanta Falcons

Football players, like prostitutes,
are in the business of ruining their bodies
for the pleasure of strangers.

MERLE KESSLER

Sport is a product of human culture.
America seems to need football at this stage
of our social development.
When you get ninety million people
watching a single game on television, it . . .
shows you that people need something
to identify with.

JOE PATERNO,

Penn State Coach

When you have a bad day,
you want to get it out of your system,
but you don't want to forget it entirely.
The thing is to get so irritated you're carried
into the next game, and you use your
irritation against the other team,
take your frustration out.

JERRY RICE,

San Francisco 49ers wide receiver

If their IQs were five points lower,
they would be geraniums.

RUSS FRANCIS,

on defensive linemen

I do believe that my best hits
border on felonious assault.

JACK TATUM

I've never known of a football writer
who ever had to stand up to a blitz.

JOE NAMATH,

N.Y. Jets quarterback

You're never out of anything,
no matter what people think.
No matter how tough the situation looks,
it's always possible to succeed,
as long as you give it an effort.

JOHN ELWAY,

Denver Broncos quarterback

Some people try to find things in this game
or put things into it which don't exist.
Football is two things.
It's blocking and tackling.

ANONYMOUS

The man who complains about the way the ball
bounces is likely the one who dropped it.

LOU HOLTZ,

U. of Arkansas football coach

My definition of a good runner is that he's
insane—he does wild things, stuff you never see,
and he does it spontaneously. Even he doesn't
know what he's going to do next.

O. J. SIMPSON,

running back

When I'm running well, my mind just goes
blank. I'm not thinking about anything at all.
Thinking is what gets you caught from behind.

O. J. SIMPSON

When everything else breaks down,
I don't hesitate to roam out of the pocket
and do the boogaloo.

FRAN TARKENTON,

Hall of Fame quarterback, inducted 1986

A school without football is in danger
of deteriorating into a medieval study hall.

VINCE LOMBARDI

Embarrassment is a great motivator.
There are some people who play very, very well
just so they don't get embarrassed in front of
their friends and a national audience.

LYNN SWANN,

Pittsburgh Steelers wide receiver

When it comes to football,
God is prejudiced—toward big, fast kids.

CHUCK MILLS

BASKETBALL

Any American boy can be a basketball star
if he grows up, up, up.

BILL VAUGHAN

The game is my wife.
It demands loyalty and responsibility,
and it gives me back fulfillment and peace.

MICHAEL JORDAN,

Chicago Bulls basketball star

Basketball games are the only place
you can yell at millionaires.

LEON THE BARBER

I just don't say it in the newspapers,
I say it in the locker room.

PATRICK EWING,

on being a team leader of the New York Knicks

The man doesn't live on Earth.
He just shows up on Earth for practice
and game days.

BOB JEFFELATO,

describing Michael Jordan

Learning how to play close to the basket
in the traditional style, that's how you
win ball games. That's how you play defense,
that's how you get high-percentage shots.
The more high-percentage shots you take,
the better your game.

KAREEM ABDUL-JABBAR

I am a good person. I haven't hurt anybody or
killed anybody. I do things to help people and
put smiles on people's faces.

DENNIS RODMAN,

on his status as a controversial player of the San Antonio Spurs

Even if I'd known why he couldn't shoot foul shots, I'd never have told him.

BILL RUSSELL,

discussing his arch-rival, Wilt Chamberlain

As a 32-year-old minor leaguer, who lacks the benefit of valuable baseball experience over the past 15 years, I am no longer comfortable that there is meaningful opportunity to continue my improvement at a satisfactory pace.

MICHAEL JORDAN

I'm back. I'm back for the love of the game.

MICHAEL JORDAN,

announcing his return to the NBA after a 17-month stint in minor league baseball

I have only three words to say about this. Thank you, baseball.

WILL PERDUE,

Chicago Bulls teammate of Michael Jordan

This is my time.
I've got to make the most of it while it's here.

REGGIE MILLER,

of the Indiana Pacers

It's always every player's goal to win a ring.
To be on a team that's the best in the world
is the ultimate.

CLYDE DREXLER

Charles couldn't wait until Michael Jordan and I
left so he could have the NBA all to himself.

MAGIC JOHNSON,

on Charles Barkley

Do I miss Charles? Yeah, like a diaper rash.

JAYSON WILLIAMS,

former teammate of Charles Barkley
on the Philadelphia 76ers

Superstars stand out, no matter
what generation they play in.

KAREEM ABDUL-JABBAR

COACHES AND MANAGERS

It isn't the size of the dog in the fight,
but the size of the fight in the dog that counts.

WOODY HAYES,

Ohio State U. football coach

Listen, if you start worrying about
the people in the stands, before too long
you're up in the stands with them.

TOM LASORDA,

L.A. Dodgers manager

There are only two kinds of coaches—those who have been fired and those who will be fired.

KEN LOEFFLER,

basketball coach

Sweat plus sacrifice equals success.

CHARLES O. FINLEY,

Oakland Athletics owner

Baseball is almost the only orderly thing in a very unorderly world. If you get three strikes, even the best lawyer in the world can't get you off.

BILL VEECK,

Chicago White Sox owner

I was in the game for love. After all, where else can an old-timer like me with one leg, who can't hear or see, live like a king while doing the only thing I wanted to do?

BILL VEECK

Cut me and I'll bleed Dodger Blue.

TOM LASORDA

Going to bed with a woman
never hurt a ball player. It's staying up all night
looking for them that does you in.

CASEY STENGEL

Good pitching will always stop good hitting,
and vice versa.

CASEY STENGEL

A coach likes to have a lot of those
old trained pigs who'll grin and jump right
in the slop for him.

DARRELL ROYAL,

U. of Texas football coach

I had no trouble communicating.
The players just didn't like what I had to say.

FRANK ROBINSON,

Cleveland Indians manager

Nobody is hurt. Hurt is in the mind.
If you can walk, you can run.

VINCE LOMBARDI

Whenever I decided to release a guy, I always had his room searched first for a gun. You couldn't take chances with some of those birds.

CASEY STENGEL

When you're playing for the national championship, it's not a matter of life or death. It's more important than that.

DUFFY DAUGHERTY,

Michigan State football coach

I probably couldn't play for me. I wouldn't like my attitude.

JOHN THOMPSON,

Georgetown basketball coach

Every winning player wants to be disciplined, but they will test you. Some guys will test you for two days, some guys will test you for a week, some guys will test you the whole year. That's why you've got to be consistent with your discipline.

BOB HILL,

San Antonio Spurs coach

If one of them jumps out of the stands
like the other night, I'd punch him out
in a Minnesota second.

BILLY MARTIN,

N.Y. Yankees manager, about Yankee Stadium fans

It's a lot tougher to be a football coach than a
President. You've got four years as President,
and they guard you. A coach doesn't have anyone
to protect him when things go wrong.

HARRY S. TRUMAN

A manager's job is simple. For 162 games you
try not to screw up all that smart stuff your
organization did last December.

EARL WEAVER,

Baltimore Orioles manager

Managing is getting paid for home runs
someone else hits.

CASEY STENGEL,

on the art of managing

Defeat is worse than death,
because you have to live with defeat.

BILL MUSSELMAN,

basketball coach

A team should be an extension of
the coach's personality.
My teams were arrogant and obnoxious.

AL MCGUIRE,

former basketball coach

I carried this fear every game.
The fear that this would be the last game I'd
ever coach. The media read me all wrong.
They thought I was arrogant. I was really just
scared. It's a great way to hide fear.

MIKE KEENAN,

coach of the St. Louis Blues

When we have a good team at Alabama,
I know it's because we have boys who come from
good Mamas and Papas.

BEAR BRYANT,

Alabama football coach

I give the same halftime speech over and over.
It works best when my players are better
than the other coach's players.

CHUCK MILLS,

Wake Forest football coach

The first year of retirement was a year of
mourning, a year of reflection and grieving.
You see, I'd spent my whole life with the game
as my main force, and when it was gone,
there was a terrible, aching hollow within me.

PAT RILEY,

L.A. Lakers coach

I think every five years every coach in the NBA
should get to take a sabbatical—a one-year paid
vacation during which you would do
just nothing, absolutely nothing.

PAT RILEY,

New York Knicks coach

The two of them deserve each other.
One's a born liar, the other's convicted.

BILLY MARTIN,

N.Y. Yankee manager, referring to Yankee star Reggie Jackson and owner George Steinbrenner

In order to keep doing what we've done,
we have to keep doing what we've done
in the past.

EARL WEAVER

I've checked my heart. I don't have one.

JOHN MCKAY,

U.S.C. Trojans coach

Coaches want to be in control.
But the people we reward for making decisions
are ultimately not in control.
When the game begins,
the athletes are on the field.

TODD CROSSETT,

former coach at Northeastern

Whew, I thought we would have to call
the fire department, my team's so hot.

CASEY STENGEL,

after his N.Y. Mets ended a 17-game losing streak

Nice guys finish last.

LEO DUROCHER,

on replacing the gentlemanly but none-too-successful Mel Ott as N.Y. Giants manager

If you aren't fired with enthusiasm,
you will be fired with enthusiasm.

VINCE LOMBARDI

It was like a heart transplant.
We tried to implant college in him
but his head rejected it.

BARRY SWITZER,

U. of Oklahoma football coach,
on player who dropped out of school

The strategy part is overrated.
Every manager tries to give his players
the chance to be successful.
Every manager I know knows that's the key.

JIM LEYLAND,

Pittsburgh Pirates manager

Not bad. Most people my age are dead.
You could look it up.

CASEY STENGEL,

asked how he was doing

Winning isn't everything,
but wanting to win is.

VINCE LOMBARDI

Show me a good loser
and I'll show you an idiot.

LEO DUROCHER

Show me a good loser
and I'll show you a loser.

UNKNOWN

No coach ever won a game by what he knows;
it's what his players have learned.

BEAR BRYANT

As men get older, the toys get more expensive.

MARVIN DAVIS,

Oakland Athletics owner,
on purchase of a professional team

You don't save a pitcher for tomorrow.
Tomorrow it may rain.

LEO DUROCHER

I never got so many questions about
my managing. I tried to get 25 guys who
didn't ask questions.

EARL WEAVER,

Baltimore Orioles Manager

It's what you learn after you know it all
that counts.

EARL WEAVER

THE LAST WORD

Sports do not build character. They reveal it.

HEYWOOD HALE BROUN

Whether it's politics or football,
winning is like shaving: you do it every day
or you wind up looking like a bum.

JACK KEMP

I always turn to the sports page first.
The sports page records people's
accomplishments; the front page has
nothing but man's failures.

EARL WARREN,

Chief Justice, U.S. Supreme Court

Sports is the toy department of human life.

HOWARD COSELL

For when the One Great Scorer comes to write against your name, He marks—not that you won or lost—but how you played the game.

GRANTLAND RICE

When the one great scorer comes to write against your name, it matters a whole hell of a lot whether you win or lose.

ATTRIBUTED TO MANY COACHES

In the field of sports you are more-or-less accepted for what you do rather than what you are.

ALTHEA GIBSON DARBON,

Wimbledon champion

Games lubricate the body and the mind.
BENJAMIN FRANKLIN

It is in games that many men
discover their paradise.
ROBERT LYND

The easiest thing in sport(s) is to win when you're good. The next easiest is to lose when you're not any good. The hardest is to lose when you're good.
That's the test of character.
ROY EISENHART

Lacrosse—boys played it first,
girls perfected it.
VALERIE BEILENSON

Confidence is the result of hours and days and weeks and years of constant work and dedication.
ROGER STAUBACH,
Dallas Cowboys quarterback

One of the greatest educational swindles ever perpetrated on American youth.

A. WHITNEY GRISWOLD,

on athletic scholarships

I was waiting for him to fall, and he'd punch me back. Talk about sassing your elders!

GEORGE FOREMAN,

heavyweight champion boxer, on his bout with Axel Schutz, 20 years his junior

Football today is far too much a sport for the few who can play it well; the rest of us, and too many of our children, get exercise from climbing up the seats in stadiums, or from walking across the room to turn on our television sets. And this is true for one sport after another, all across the board.

JOHN F. KENNEDY

If I ever needed a brain transplant,
I'd choose a sportswriter because I'd want
a brain that had never been used.

NORM VAN BROCKLIN

Arrogant, pompous, obnoxious, vain, cruel,
verbose, a showoff. I have been called all of these.
Of course, I am.

HOWARD COSELL,
sportscaster

Being a sports fan is a complex matter,
in part irrational . . . but not unworthy . . .
a relief from the seriousness of the real world,
with its unending pressures and
often grave obligations.

RICHARD GILMAN

Anyone who will tear down sports will tear
down America. Sports and religion have made
America what it is today.

WOODY HAYES